A Selection of Drawings of Ivybridge and the Surrounding Villages

By Luthfi Gulliver

The **First and Last** public house, Ermington, on entering from the north side.

This version of the book is virtually as originally published, presenting the work of Luthfi Gulliver. There are now additional pages at the back providing information about the publisher, Arthur L Clamp.

The republishing project is being managed by Arthur's grandson, Steven Gibson. We aim to find all the research that he was involved in publishing, preserving it for the next generation as part of 'The Clamp Collection'.

INTRODUCTION

Ivybridge is situated on the River Erme and to the southernmost tip of Dartmoor. It is in close proximity to the A38 dual carriageway between Plymouth and Exeter, and is the fastest growing town in the South Hams.

Along with much of the surrounding area the original village dates back to the Domesday survey of 1086 when there was a ford over the River Erme which marked the divisions of the four parishes it served. By the thirteenth or fourteenth century this was replaced by a bridge built with its four corners each in one of these parishes and was, until recently, overgrown with ivy, hence it's name.

Ugborough is to the east and is an historically interesting village which was built around an ancient earth works, while Ermington, to the south, with its old mill and crooked church spire standing over the square is particularly picturesque and seems almost to have been over-looked by the twentieth century.

The mill at Lee Mill, west of Ivybridge, is now used as a warehouse and the shop or two and public house which make up the village itself is divided by a busy highway. A new industrial estate and a large supermarket are situated on the Ivybridge side.

To either side of the narrow Harford Road which runs for three miles along the edge of Dartmoor are the isolated farm and stone buildings which make up the parish of Harford. The church and the school house lie half way along the road which eventually runs into Cornwood, a charming village itself surrounded by a scattering of smaller villages.

Ivybridge is now a thriving and growing town. The old mills, many of the farms and much of the older traditions are already gone, and there is much change on the way. I have recorded in my drawings various parts of the town and the surrounding villages in the hope that they will capture something of this time of transition in the history of Ivybridge.

Luthfi Gulliver,
11 Crossways,
Cornwood, Ivybridge,
South Devon.

The Artist and Author

Luthfi Gulliver moved to the Ivybridge area in 1985 having spent part of his early years in the Far East. He is attending the Plymouth College of Art and Design studying Graphic Design but at weekends and during vacations he can be found walking and recording what he sees through his line drawings and notes. A keen observer of what goes on around him, he wishes to share his love of the Ivybridge area and has worked towards this end through this publication. It is his first venture into book illustration which suitably complements his student work in Plymouth.

Costly Street in Ivybridge with Highland Street running in the background.

London Hotel as viewed from Station Road with the old river bridge.

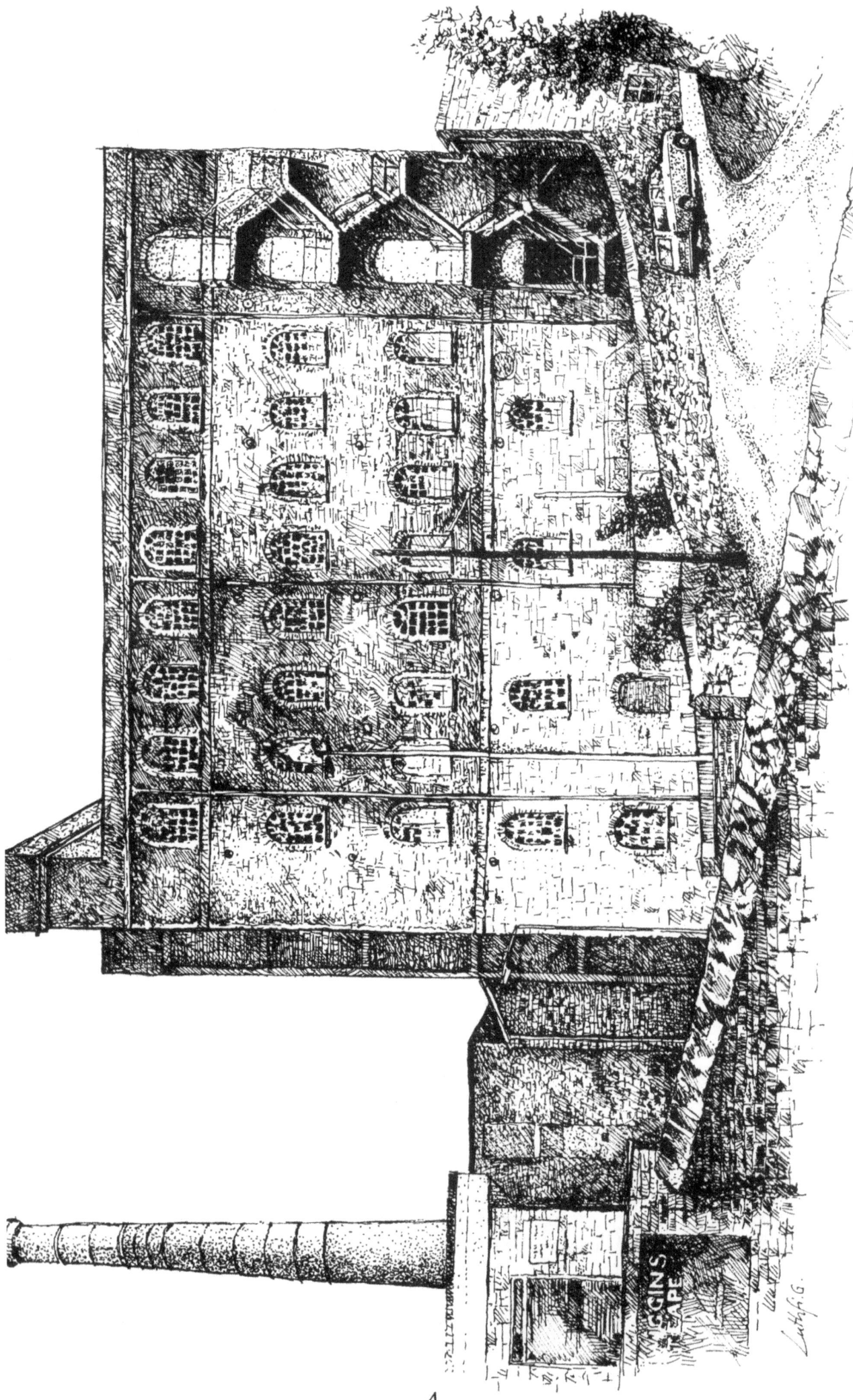

The Wiggins Teape large papermill at Ivybridge seen in its two hundredth year of working.

Some of the many shops in Fore Street, Ivybridge.

Bernard Lawrence's general engineering workshop at the rear of Fore Street, Ivybridge.

The Town Dairy in the Fore Street, Ivybridge.

Bowden's Garage, Western Road, Ivybridge.

The First and Second World War Memorial with Exeter Road running east.

The stone built Allen's Cottages, Fore Street, Ivybridge.

The former Wesleyan Chapel in Ivybridge which was converted into the Town Hall in 1978.

The **Exchange** public house, formerly the **King's Arms**, in the Fore Street, Ivybridge.

The South Devon Leisure Centre, Ivybridge, opened in April, 1987.

Part of the old 1860 railway water system in Crescent Road, Ivybridge.

St. John's Church, Blatchford Road, Ivybridge.

Sixty-eight steps leading to Ivybridge's former Great Western Railway station.

The original 18th century Woodlands Manor. The only listed building in Ivybridge in process of being converted into flats.

Old Woodland's cemetery; the names and descriptions on the different stones tell much of old Ivybridge.

Ivybridge from Ermington Road with Western Beacon in the background.

Boringdon Park, Ivybridge, part of a new estate built in 1987 on the outskirts of the town.

Stowford railway bridge, Coles Lane, at Harford Road crossways.

A general view of Stowford Farm and reservoir standing above Ivybridge.

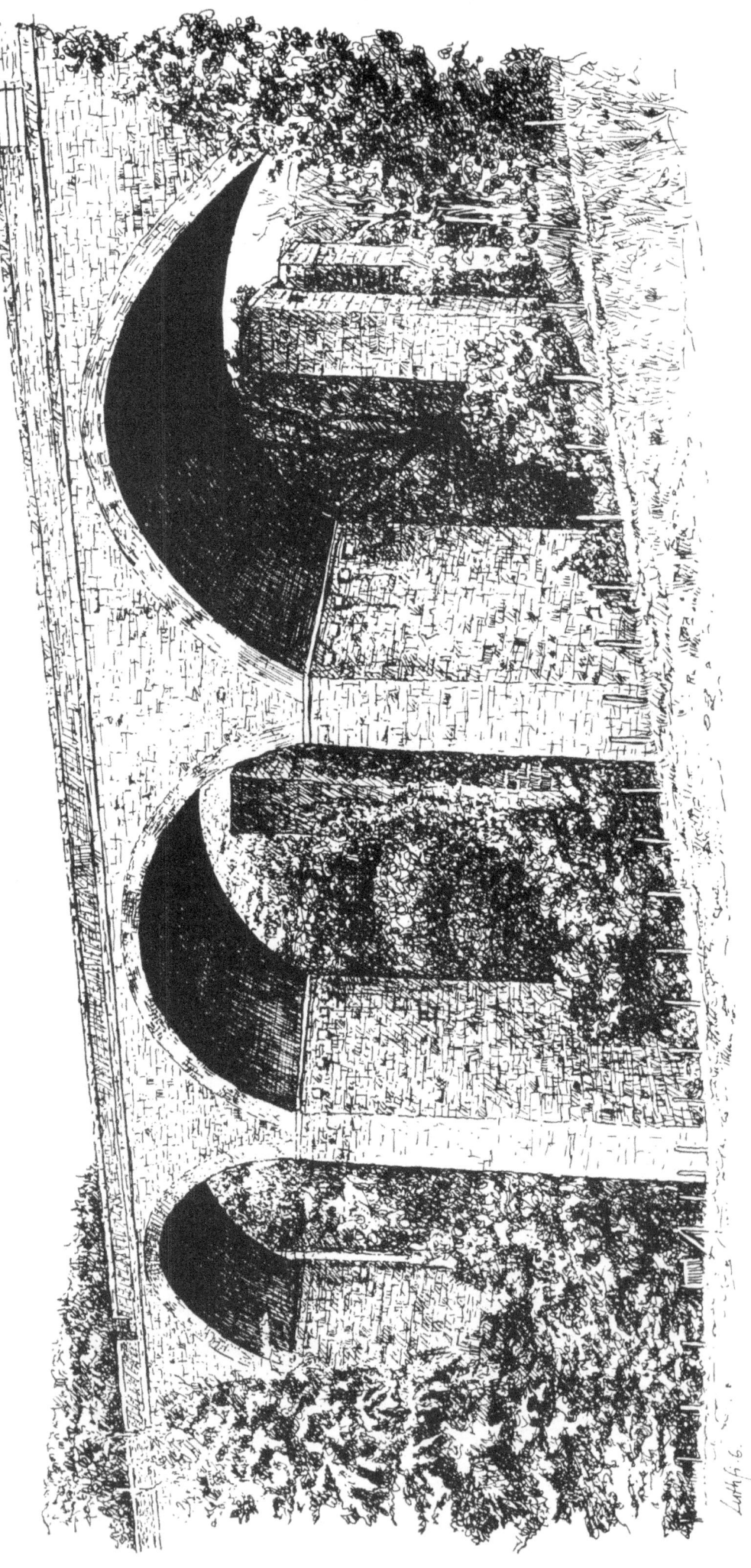

Brunel's old broad-gauge railway viaduct columns standing below the later railway bridge. The broad-gauge track was lifted in 1892.

The old courtyard at Stowford Farmhouse, Harford. Site of the original kitchen with a steeple chimney dating from 1482.

One of the many Bronze Age stone hut circles on the moor above Harford.

The moorstone Harford church which dates from the late 15th-16th century.

The cobbled yard at Hall Farm, Harford, a typical Dartmoor farm on the edge of the high moor dating from 1600.

Bond Street with some of its cottages in Cornwood.

The original blacksmith's building, mounting steps and smithy cottage in the Square at Cornwood.

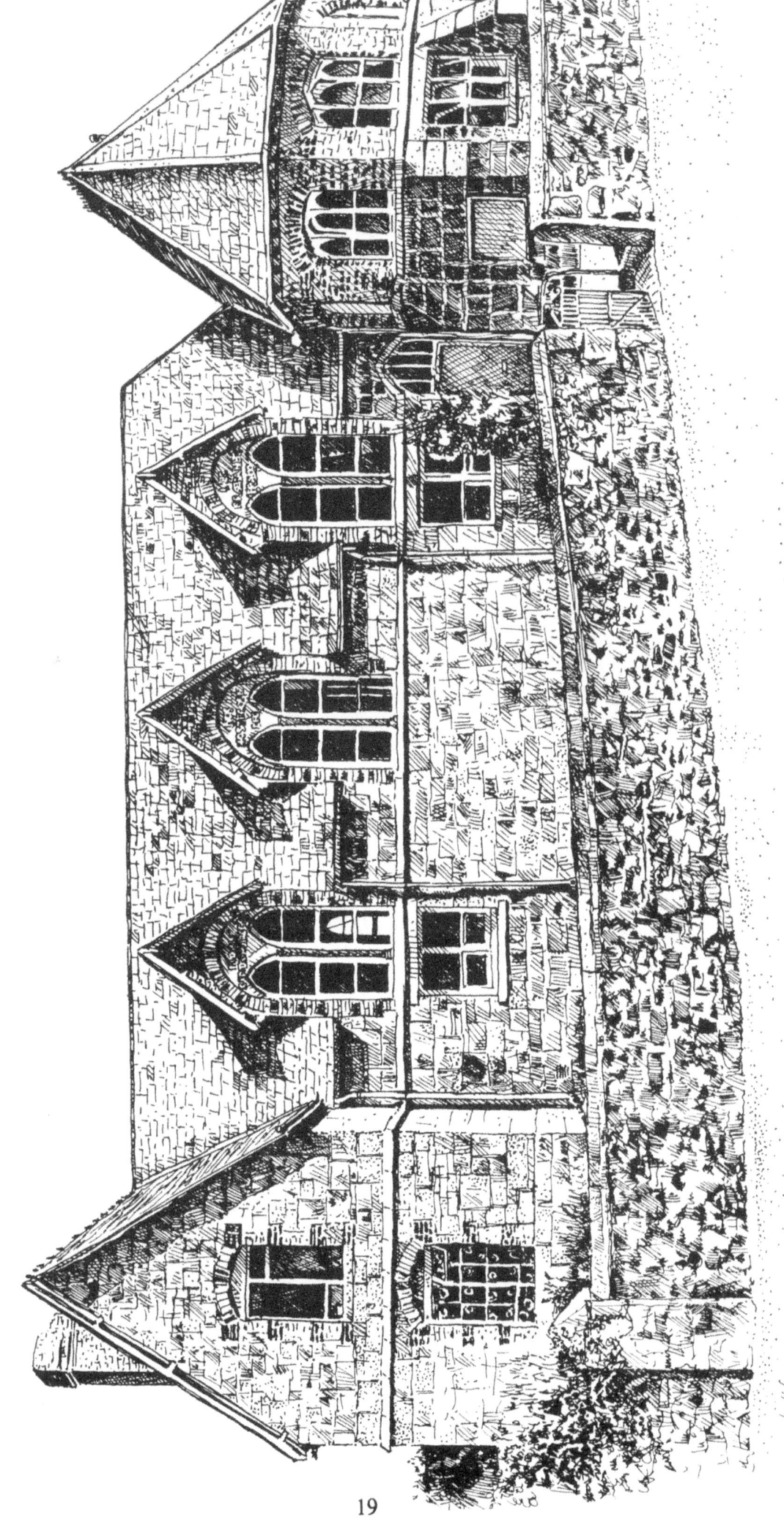

Cornwood Primary School, dated 1859, a substantial moorstone building in the village.

The modern Tesco's shopping centre at Lee Mill.

An enamelled billplate at Lee Mill, now a rare sight.

The old mill and chimney at Lee Mill, once a papermill, now occupied by Harris's, engineers.

The 94ft. high tower of St. Peter's Church, Ugborough, overlooks the whole village.

Two rugged Dartmoor ponies feeding on the slopes of Western Beacon above Ivybridge.

The old Red Lake quarry china clay drying sheds now occupied by the Western Machinery and Equipment Company.

Bittaford railway viaduct with the **Horse and Groom** just beyond.

Ermington Mill was established in 1820 and is now used as a craft centre.

A view of the Trout Farm at Ermington Mill which opened in 1972.

A milestone on Exeter Road, dating from the years of the Turnpike Trusts.

The church of St. Peter and St Paul, Ermington, well known for its crooked spire.

Arthur L. Clamp – the man behind the books

Arthur Leslie Clamp was a man of boundless energy with a passion for helping others, particularly through his love of history. A printer by trade, he started his career in a printing company before moving his family from Exeter to Plymouth to teach at the Plymouth College of Art and Design, where he eventually became the Head of the Printing Department.

A Devoted Family Man

Arthur with his five children.

Despite his love of teaching, Arthur prioritised his family, always making it home by 5:30pm for tea. He and his wife, Rosemary, raised five children: Susan, Angela, Elizabeth, David, and Steven. Arthur would often combine his love of family and history by taking his children on Sunday walks, encouraging them to appreciate historical monuments by taking photos or making crayon rubbings of gravestones for his books. The family home at 203 Elburton Road was a hub of activity, with a large garden, featuring a two-storey fort and a makeshift swimming pool.

A Lifelong Learner and Adventurer

Arthur's thirst for knowledge extended beyond history to a deep curiosity about the world. He was passionate about exploring different cultures, traditions, and cuisines, often taking advantage of his long summer holidays as a teacher to travel to places like India, Russia, South America, the middle east and the USA, sometimes bringing one of his children along. This adventurous spirit even influenced his home life, as seen by the short-lived family tradition of steam-cooking vegetables after a trip to Iceland.

History is a prominent feature of family days out

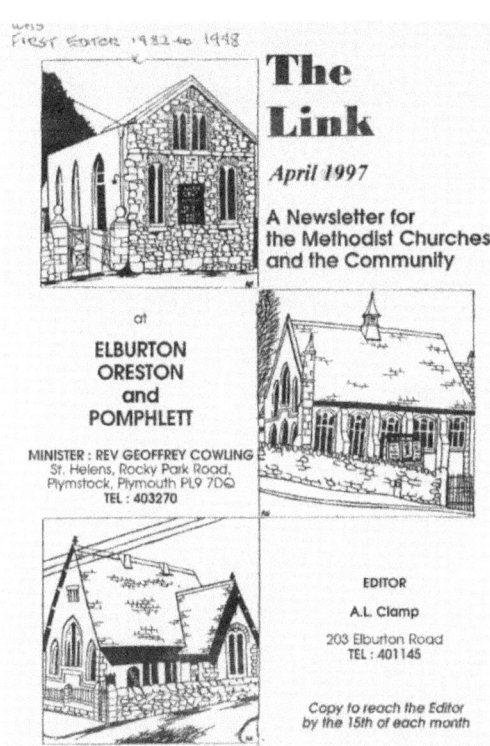

Community and Philanthropic Spirit

His commitment to serving others was evident in his long-standing involvement with the Elburton Methodist Church. He was the Sunday School Superintendent for over 15 years and served as the editor of the wider church's monthly newsletter, "The Link," for a similar duration. After Rosemary's very sad passing, Arthur later remarried and, following a chance encounter with a professor from India, established a connection with a missionary school in Chennai. Together with his new wife, Christine, he co-founded a "Sponsor a Child's Education" program that continues to this day.

*Pictured left – The cover of 'The Link' complete
with hand drawn sketches of each church by Angela
Below right – Arthur Clamp promoting his latest book
Below left – Arthur at home with his first wife, Rosemary
Below centre – Arthur on holiday with his second wife,
Christine*

A Legacy of Learning and Positivity

Arthur's greatest passion was history, which he brought to life through tireless research, documentation, and the many books he authored. He was driven by a need to "never be stuck in a rut," constantly seeking new experiences, meeting new people, and expanding his knowledge. With a positive attitude and a great sense of humour, he was always ready to help others, leaving a lasting impact on his family and community. His children, Susan, Angela, Elizabeth, David, and Steven, remember him with love and gratitude.

David Clamp, 2025

A Legacy of Local History

Below is the story of how Arthur L Clamp began writing books, in his own words, drafted shortly before he passed away in 2001. I have only made minor alterations to this text, correcting grammatical errors that he did not survive to correct himself. When I first discovered this text, I was shocked to see my name mentioned. It seems that, unbeknownst to me, I shared my first PC with him. I suspect he used it during the day when I was at school, although I do have one memory of sitting with him and showing him how it worked. It has been a pleasure to pick up where he left off and see his books republished and redistributed, and to know that I was part of the story, even back then. It was also fascinating to discover that his pricing structure matches the way I have tried to price the books, with a third going to local sellers and the rest covering printing costs with a little left over for my expenses.

I am his eldest grandson, and it is a privilege to curate his legacy, which we are calling 'The Clamp Collection'. The very last line of the text originally reads "The following pages list all the titles." Sadly, that page is missing and we have no record of all the books he published and knowing that some of those were researched by other authors makes the process of finding them even harder. I look forward to one day completing the collection and seeing them all available again. And maybe, one day, I'll even start writing my own to add to the series. For now, here is his story in his own words.

Steven Gibson, 2025

Writing and Publishing Booklets on Local Topics and Areas

I started this interest in either 1968 or 1969 when living in Woodford. I had by these dates established the Department of Printing and I think I must have been looking for something different to do. The first titles were of A5 size proofed from type set at Clarke, Doble and Brendon, Ltd., Plymouth printers, and then made up into pages and printed at Sawtell and Neilson, Ltd., Totnes.

Then began a slow process of getting them out to shops, etc. which proved to be more time consuming and difficult than actually researching, writing and getting the books into print. However, I persisted and opened a business account with Barclays Bank on the Broadway. I was advised to give it a title so I called it "Westway Publications". There came along another problem, one of storage of paper and finished books which was solved when the family moved to Elburton in 1970.

I changed the printer to Penwell, Ltd., Callington, Cornwall, as he was then just setting up himself and his prices seemed very reasonable. I did not get any of the printers to make up the complete books. I hand folded the flat printed sheets, stitched the books on a small manual table stitcher and trimmed them in a small hand turned guillotine which I bought from someone in Penzance for £40. It was brought up in a van.

The trouble and time going to and fro to Callington was too much so I transferred the printing to PDS Printers, Prince Rock, Plymouth, and I have been with them ever since. Now they are at Plympton which is easy to reach and they fold the flat sheets which was turning out to be a long chore which only saved a small part of the printing costs.

All my first titles were written by myself. I took the photographs and developed them in the loft of the house, the type was set by now on a computer situated in the house at Elburton from which I had collected photographic lengths of text to cut up and law down as pages.

At some point I decided that I would do my own film processing of lith film so I bought a large second hand process camera from Kingsbridge and learnt through trial and error to make line negatives of the text and halftone negatives of the illustrations which proved more difficult than I anticipated. The main problem was trying to keep the developer in the large dish at the correct temperature as any change would affect the developing time. I replaced this old camera with a brand new one bought from Croydon, Surrey, costing £900. This has turned out to be a great asset cutting out an expensive part of the printer's costs and one crucial aspect of the work which I could control.

By the middle 1970s there were many outlets I had contacted in Plymouth, up to Dartmoor, Exeter, around to Torbay, Totnes, Dartmouth and the South Hams. The market for local books was much greater than I had first thought and through getting to know many local people undertaking research themselves had the chance to help and make up books for other people who had in most instances, got together a collection of photographs with some text in a rather muddled way. Through my experience in print I was able to shape up their work and get it into print and in every case I had to pay the printer and let the person have the royalties. In the majority of titles produced in this manner this was another way of producing titles and it did give some profit to my work. However, I must say that in a few cases I lost out by either the other person getting the numbers wrong, not returning any monies from stock I delivered or they thought that more of their books should have been sold.

The print run was usually 1,000 copies and from time to time I have had reprints of 250 copies. It took about ten years to clear the first print run so I always had large stocks in the garage, workshop, etc. The numbers sold during the early years was about 7,000 copies a year increasing to around 9,000 copies and for the whole of the enterprise about 500,000 have been sold. The booklets have become part of the local scene and many people collect them, shops regularly order copies and I go around certain areas month by month restocking or replacing titles as necessary.

During the past year or so I have started setting the text on a Packard Bell PC, something which I should have done some years back. I share it with Steven Gibson, my grandson. There appears to be no end to the market for local books, but I could not earn a regular income because of the long time it takes to sell stock.

However, now exceeding 100 titles made up mainly of A4 twenty-four page booklets, some folded guides, with selling prices set with a third going to the shop which is the trade custom, the original idea has been quite successful and could go on for ever.

Apart from monetary benefits, however spasmodically these might be, I have learnt a lot myself, met many interesting people and have become part of the local scene with requests to give talks and to advise people about getting into print.

Arthur L Clamp, 2001

This newspaper article, published by the Evening Herald on 17th August 2001, forms a good record of his life. Just as he encourages us to learn more about local history, we encourage you to learn a little about him. For that reason, we have included these pages at the back of all the most recently republished books, in honour of his memory and recognition of his contribution to the community.

www.ingramcontent.com/pod-product-compliance
Lightning Source LLC
Chambersburg PA
CBHW061406070526
44584CB00031B/4173